On the Cusp

A Fourth Book of
Thought Provoking Poems

Liz Mingo

Copyright © 2025 Liz Mingo

All rights reserved, including the right to reproduce this book, or portions thereof in any form. No part of this text may be reproduced, transmitted, downloaded, decompiled, reverse engineered, or stored, in any form or introduced into any information storage and retrieval system, in any form or by any means, whether electronic or mechanical without the express written permission of the author.

ISBN: 978-1-917778-51-0

Other books by this author

POETRY

Between Green and Orange
Thought Provoking Poems

Hello Yellow
A Second Book of Thought Provoking Poems

Le Troisième
A Third Book of Thought Provoking Poems

SHORT STORIES

Tom and Laurie

Who Am I?

I was born in the Commonwealth of Dominica, West Indies. I came to England in 1975, a very shy 10-year-old! I started writing in the late 80's after being prompted by a friend. I didn't take my writing seriously until much later. As I got older, my poems were influenced by events that were happening in everyday life and, being reported on the news, and by issues experienced by family and friends. I would describe my poetry as a bag of liquorice allsorts - you will laugh, cry, think, start a debate, maybe even relate!

From my head, to my fingers, to the page, to your mind, to your body, to your soul!

I can be contacted on Instagram: @lizm4000.

Thank You

To my family, nothing but love, always.

To my friends, thank you for the continued support and encouragement.

Thank you to everyone who inspired a poem in this collection, albeit knowingly or unknowingly. From family and friends, to the stranger in the Park who gave me the idea for The Park Bench.

Remembering Uncles Nassief and Ezol from the Mingo Family Tree. Resting, and at peace.

It's a Joy!

Contents

1. All Over Me 1
2. Alone 2
3. At the End of My Ink 3
4. A Forever We Cannot See 4
5. A Longing for Love 5
6. Belonging 6
7. Be Gone! 7
8. Can't Stop Thinking About You 8
9. Catching Stars 9
10. Choose To Forget 10
11. Cutting Edge 11
12. Cut Short 13
13. Daily Quote (1) 15
14. Daily Quote (2) 16
15. Daily Quote (3) 17
16. Daily Quote (4) 18
17. Dancing in Rainstorms 19

18. Did You?..20

19. Don't Touch My...22

20. Empty Eyes...23

21. Everywhere...25

22. Falling Without Cause 26

23. Feeling Fabulous at 50 – A Menopause Journey.......27

24. Full of Love 28

25. Gone Too Soon...29

26. Home...30

27. Hot Flashes – A Menopause Journey 31

28. Ice 32

29. If I Could Call Heaven..33

30. I Know... 35

31. I'm Here 36

32. I Met Someone...37

33. I Was Never Yours 38

34. Kissing You With The Lights On............................39

35. Letter to the Black Man 40

36. Love Me Like… 43

37. Love, Not Sex 44
38. Men Cry Too 46
39. Midnight Poetry 47
40. One Last Dance 48
41. One Touch 50
42. Pick Me! 51
43. Poems Never Written 52
44. Poem to a Stranger 53
45. Poetic Scars 55
46. Postcard 56
47. Secret 57
48. She Walks in Beauty 58
49. Side Effects of Poetry 59
50. Soundtrack of Memories 60
51. Stop 61
52. Suffer the Little Children 63
53. Tell Me How To Love You 65
54. The Date 66
55. The Hotel 67

56. The Keepsake 69

57. The Park Bench 70

58. To My Future Love 71

59. Toothpaste and Orange 72

60. Unique 74

61. What Love is (1) 76

62. What Love Is (2) 78

63. When I Say What I Say 79

64. Why Did You Tell Me? 80

65. Why Me – A Menopause Journey 82

66. Willing 83

67. Yes, You Can! 84

68. You Are the Story 85

All Over Me

The way you look at me
Is just how I imagined.
Not gonna lie,
Been dreaming about this for some time,
And now, here we are:
Body to body, skin to skin,
Your hands all over me;
Searching,
Probing,
Longing to do naughty things.
They part my thighs;
Fingers fondle my privates
And start to stimulate.
The temperature's rising,
Your dick stands to attention –
Ready for action.
On all fours,
I'm all yours,
And as my face cracks a smile,
You hit me doggy style.

Alone

[Trigger warning: sexual assault]

They left me alone
With this man.
I remember his hands
All over me.
I was sick to my stomach,
Tried to shake him off
But he was way too strong.
Tried to run
But he had me pinned down.
He was bigger and stronger
And should have known better
But he did it anyway.
I remember the pain.
So much pain!
I remember the blood.
So much blood!
I prayed he'd never do it again
But he did.
He thought I was older,
But I was only 12
When he raped me.

At the End of My Ink

At the end of my ink
A story will have been written;
One about you and me.
It won't be long, or complicated;
It will be direct, and succinct.
It will tell how you entered my life and gave it meaning,
How I wake up each day, face beaming,
And most of all,
By the end of my ink,
Our hearts shall beat in sync.

A Forever We Cannot See

We say we love,
But is love enough?
Yin and yang,
Darkness and light,
Half full, half empty.
There's a forever we cannot see,
Because you and me
Can never agree.

A Longing for Love

Once bitten, twice shy.
So I locked it away
Deliberately,
Shielded my broken heart
From another attack.
It was time to take care of me,
Give myself space to grieve, but
This itch needs to be scratched.
So, at long last
I'm ready!
Hungry, and thirsty, and burning
With a desire for love again.

Belonging
[Trigger warning: abuse]

I hated that he had this hold on me,
This authority.
Always had me backed into a corner,
And I told him exactly what he wanted to hear.
All done out of fear, and a longing for safety
To escape the clutches of this monster!
I was a slave to his rhythm
For far too long,
Succumbing to his every threat.

I needed to show him I wasn't weak.
Lose the safety net;
Cut the apron strings;
Things were going to be different from here on in.
So, when he asked again,
I told him,
In my own voice, no whimper...
"I belong to me, you punk ass motherfucker!"

Be Gone!

There's the door,
Please leave.
Had enough of your sorry ass!
Kicking myself for being so dumb, and
Not seeing what was clearly looking back at me,
You!
A pathetic, worthless mess.
Dude, be gone!
Fact is,
I've had enough;
You simply have to leave.
No more ifs, buts, or maybes,
It's time. You need to bounce!
No more doors left slightly open
Or glasses half full,
I'm done being your fool.
So, before my self-esteem depreciates,
There's the door.
I'd appreciate you leaving quietly.

Can't Stop Thinking About You

It's constant, all the time;
In fact, every second,
You occupy my mind 24/7, 365,
Can't hide.
When you're not here, it's torture.
I'm your biggest supporter,
You're my champion.
You fill every empty space,
Cure every ache,
I love you with a passion!
You blinker my vision.
Never thought I'd be affected like this
All day, every day,
Your kiss, your embrace,
The way your hands caress my face.
I daydream,
Have wet dreams;
They will have to do
Until I'm home with you.

Catching Stars

...And I'll catch the stars for you
Even if you don't ask me to.
I'd catch much more than just stars
To see the look in your eyes,
To have you embrace me,
To hear your heart beating loudly.
'Cause then, I'd be where I wanted to be!

Choose To Forget

If you chose to forget me,
My tears would flow like a tsunami.
My cheeks would swell,
My eyes would be all puffy.
Yet I would deserve it
For all the lies,
All the cheating,
All the shame I have caused.
So, if you choose to forget me,
I will not hold it against you.

Cutting Edge
[Trigger warning: self-harm]

The first time was instinctive.
It was just there: the blade.
So fucking frustrated,
I needed to release,
So, I used it!
Screamed at the top of my voice
When I saw the blood.
All over the bathroom floor,
The sink,
It was mine!
The bathroom was a mess.
I needed to assess,
Make sense of what just happened.
This wasn't me, surely!?
Was this my reality?
That, as of today,
Once shit hit the fan, I'd be reaching…
For a blade!
Can't lie, but
After that first time,
Cutting was easy.
Didn't want it to be my identity, but
It happened with regularity.

Once everything got too much
I'd cut, and cut, and cut.
It gave me relief;
It allowed me to breathe;
My body felt empty,
Ready for the next wave of anxiety.
Then I'd cut again, and again, and again.
Never actually felt any pain.
Guess I became immune.
Allowed the blade to take control,
Danced to its tune,
Oblivious to the fact that I was falling…
Overwhelmed,
Distressed,
Knee-deep,
Now a statistic.
I carry a label,
I'm marked for life,
'Cause these scars can't hide;
They're in full view,
Acting as a reminder
That whatever life throws at you,
Self-harming is not the answer.

Cut Short

[Trigger warning: violence, misogyny]

There was such joy!
Cut short, sadly,
Her life ended, abruptly –
Another jealous partner.
Sick of this!
These weak men
Playing dirty.
Sometimes bringing jack shit
To the party, yet
Wanna be dancing like crazy!
Playing happy families,
But it's all bullshit;
False sense of security.
This has sincerely angered me!
Just one sistren too many.
There's a lot going on right now,
But this one's on my radar.
Had to give it my attention,
So picked up a pen
To release some frustration.
These innocent women –
Rebecca Cheptegei,
Damaris Muthee Mutua,
Agnes Tirop,

What the fuck!
When is this shit gonna stop?
Homicide by Femicide.
Women give life,
Yet theirs are taken.
Chauvinistic,
Narcissistic
Misogynists.
Enough is enough!
Time to bring these cowards to justice.

Daily Quote (1)

Sometimes, people just gotta let you be, and vice versa.

Daily Quote (2)

It isn't necessary to beat yourself up
If everything isn't as right as rain on the daily.
Some days will be better than others.
Allow yourself to feel how you feel.

Daily Quote (3)

The hardest part is acknowledging there's a problem. That's half the battle won.
Let's go!

Daily Quote (4)

No matter how much others may big you up and try to influence you,
Ultimately, it starts with You.

Dancing in Rainstorms

Umbrellas lost
They serve no purpose now
Not in this storm
We're soaked through
Yet hardly notice
Uggs ruined beyond repair
We're Rogers and Astaire
Minus the fancy shoes
Dancing on the street
Wet socks on our feet
The heavens remain open
Heavy rain falling from the sky
We close our eyes
We spin and twirl and twirl and spin
We couldn't care less who is watching
Let them think us crazy
'Cause until this storm subsides
We'll continue to dance.

Did You?

Going behind my back,
Ducking and diving,
Letting her in,
Giving her access to your body.
Her hands caressing
And tracing
Every curve;
Her lips kissing
Every old scar.
You enter her,
Pleasure her,
Moaning and groaning
Until the final act
Of climax.
And now, here we are,
Me saying *au revoir*
While you're sat in the corner, crying,
Playing the victim,
Naw, this ain't washing.
You betrayed;
You deceived;
I should be peed –
Not you!
My love was 100,
But not anymore

So, there's the door,
Please exit.
'Cause when you consented to this,
You didn't think about me.
Did you?

Don't Touch My...

How long must we endure this
Discrimination,
Your fascination,
Question after question?
Must we continually repeat
Again and again and again?
Do you not hear us?
We know you curious
'Cause we always got a different style;
It's just that our hair is versatile.
Enough is enough, 'cause
We tired!
You can look, but
For the record, and
Just so the message is clear –
No, you can't touch my goddamn hair!

Empty Eyes
[Trigger warning: mental illness]

I look at her, sat there.
My friend.
Her eyes say
She's a million miles away.
Not sure what brought this on, but
Whatever it is, weighs heavy.
Was it friends?
Was it family?
Was it society?
Her wanting to please so much,
She's now lost the plot.
Out of touch –
Mind and body out of sync.
It's a hard watch.
She needs to talk, but it's tricky,
How do I approach this?
Anxiety written all over her face.
I'm praying she doesn't break;
I'm praying she gathers strength;
I'm praying she comes out the other side.
I'm no medic
So, until she can get the help she needs,
I offer a safe space:

An ear, a shoulder,
Patience, understanding,
Empathy.
None of us are exempt.

Everywhere

Everywhere I look, you're there.
I cannot look right nor left
Without stopping and catching my breath.
You're the glint in my eyes,
Permanent,
Here to stay, and
I wouldn't have it any other way.

Falling Without Cause

It's rapid!
Uncontrollable.
I'm falling,
That's clear,
Yet I cannot put my finger on the reason.
It's rapid!
Uncontrollable,
Unexplainable.
I'm falling without cause, yet
I'm not even scared.
I'm not calling, or bawling, or shouting;
I'm snowballing.
Yet I find it therapeutic, and enthralling.

Feeling Fabulous at 50 – A Menopause Journey

Hell yeah,
And why not!
Just 'cause you've hit the Five Zero
Don't mean you gotta wallow
In self-pity,
And be
All sorrow-ful and shitty.
It's time to get jiggy,
To celebrate, to party,
Paint the town blue or white or red,
Hell, you ain't dead!
So get out there:
The world is your oyster,
And you're a gem.
Forget them –
Those who say you're too old to...
Get on up, strut your stuff,
Show the world you all that, and then some.
Let rip like you on a home run
'Cause Queen, you 50 and
Fab-U-Lous!

Full of Love

Bon appétit!
That phrase is on repeat.
The plate of food is in front of me:
Mac and cheese;
Fries, with mushy peas;
Mash potato;
Avocados;
All my favourites.
This plate is all gravy!
So, what's wrong with me?
I am so full of love,
I can barely eat.
Bon appétit!

Gone Too Soon

She was taken.
Makes no sense to me.
Trying to make the pieces add up,
Fit into place,
Someway, somehow,
But maybe they don't and shouldn't.
She was taken.
And way too soon.
Too soon for her friends and family,
So unexpected; such a tragedy!
But if her number was up...
It may never make sense,
But we need to accept
She was taken,
Find a way to move on,
And make sure she's never forgotten.

Home

Arms wrapped around me
Gently,
Yet ever so tight.
Loved up and cosy.
Cheeks all rosy.
Hearts beating in tandem...
Home is you!

Hot Flashes – A Menopause Journey

Let's not beat about the bush,
When the heat is on, it's on!
Although it's temporary,
It's sudden.
The worst thing about the flash?
It hits when you least expect.
It's intense.
The face, the chest, the neck,
All hot and sweaty,
Then you come over all chilly.
It's bizarre.
And annoying too,
But, like all the other symptoms,
A hot flash doesn't last!
Ain't no place to hide
So, best to just run with it.
You're woman. You got this!

Ice

You, cold
Your heart, frozen
Words, unspoken
You, enticing
Inviting
Foreplay
Breaking the Ice

If I Could Call Heaven...

Hell, I'd jump at the chance!
Man, that would be something.
Impossible to put a time on
How long I'd stay talking.
What I can say for certain
Is that I'd be selfish;
I would need an unlimited tariff –
Pay-As-You-Go just wouldn't cut it!
The first voice I'd wanna hear is my Granny.
She raised me.
So, there's a bond...
I talk to her every day anyway
(At least to the photo in my room),
But to have her respond?
Hear those silky, smooth tones again,
Oh my goodness!
Would I even be able to speak?
My eyes would well up;
Tears would salt my cheeks.
Not sure I'd be able to stop crying –
Tears of joy, of course.
Would probably need to put down,
Then pick up;
Compose myself...
I'd rot her ears,

Telling her about things I've done
And things she's missed out on.
Hello, Heaven, this may take a while...
I'd ask Granny to fetch the Uncles,
The Aunties, other family members,
And my Mummy!
I'd tell her about my achievements,
And hope she'd be proud of me.
I would then... Hello? Hello?
Heaven, can you hear me?
Hello,
Hello! ...
Hadn't banked on cloud interference.
What a nuisance!
Is there a telephone engineer up there?

I Know...

I know you want me.
I know you want to
Hold me,
Caress me,
Kiss me,
Touch me
In places reserved for lovers, but
These feelings make no sense
'Cause you're my friend.
This is driving me insane!
'Cause I know you know
I feel exactly the same.

I'm Here

I hope you know this.
We've been friends for too long
For you not to.
I wanna make the first move, but
That should be up to you.
I can see through the pretence,
I can smell the bullshit.
Stop playing tough and admit it!
I see the pain you're in,
I know you're hurting.
So please, stop faking.
No more lies; bring the facts.
Stop being the clown;
No-one is laughing,
So quit!
Time to shed the skin
You've surrounded yourself in.
Time to come clean,
Only then can the healing process begin.
So, when you're ready,
I'm here for you!

I Met Someone

It may have been a Monday
Or a Tuesday, or even a Wednesday –
The day isn't important.
What I remember, and vividly,
Was the way you walked towards me.
Tall and dark and handsome.
The sun shone ever so brightly.
My heart skipped beats,
My cheeks,
Hot and rosy,
Glowing,
Butterflies fluttering.
We locked eyes
And in that moment, I knew
You were the one!

I Was Never Yours

I see the hurt in your eyes,
And I apologise,
I sincerely do.
But it was always YOU and ME,
Never US,
So why the fuss about the breakup?
This was never meant to be serious,
Just a temporary thing,
A fling!
I thought you understood that.
My heart never skipped beats;
There were never butterflies in my stomach.
I made sure not to give off the wrong signals, too,
'Cause I never wanted to hurt you.
Not sure how, but you gotta get over this,
'Cause I was never yours to fall in love with.

Kissing You With The Lights On

Too in love to care
This ain't no dare
Just time to be true
All eyes on us
Don't care too much for the fuss
Nothing to discuss
Breaking with tradition
No more stealing kisses
Or making love in the dark
I want to kiss you with the lights on
Wanna see every scar you say is ugly
Every pimple
Want the lights to show off the real you
You're way too beautiful to hide
So slide even closer
And let me kiss you some more

Letter to the Black Man

Dear Black Man,

We see you.
Looking all confused.
Consumed by self-doubt,
Brought on by issues from your childhood
Which haven't been resolved.

We know you've had it tough
Being told to
Man Up,
Stand Tall,
Get Over It,
Don't Cry,
Take It Like a Man.
So you do.
'Cause you refuse to show weakness.

Society demands you act tough,
Yet still expects to see
Softness,
Vulnerability,
You at your lowest,
In tune with your feminine side,
Tears falling from your eyes

Yet,
"Real men don't cry," right!

Society expects you to act
This way, but not that;
Be that way, but not this;
Show this side, but not that.
And though your head
May be ready to explode
Due to the heavy load,
You're expected to be
Robust, yet cool, and
How dare you not comply?
"Real men can't break," right!

Dear Black Man,
We know you exhausted.
So, enough is enough.
Hang tough.
Take a load off.
Showing insecurities
Will not hamper your abilities, so
Cry if you need to.
Embrace your pain.
Wipe away the shame.
Give society the finger;
Own your trauma.
No more suppressing.
No more depression.

Bid it all *adieu*, and start anew.
'Cause, dear Black Man,
We see you!

Yours Lovingly,
The Black Woman.

Love Me Like…

Love me like you've never loved before,
Like I'm your first;
Love me like you need to quench a thirst.
Ride me like I'm a streetcar named desire,
Baby, ignite my fire!
Turn the passion up full throttle.
No rations here,
So, if you're hungry, eat me.
Spread honey over my body,
And lick to your heart's content.
Love me like I'm the latest trend,
Love me like the world's about to end!

Love, Not Sex

Make love to me
Don't sex me!
Do naughty things to my body
Your tongue is the key
Unlock me sensually
Make me scream with ecstasy
Let your hands caress
And stroke me
Intensely!
Passionately!
You're my desire
Ignite my fire
Keep the flames burning
Plant kiss after kiss
On my already wet lips
Fingertips
My clit!
Senses awakened
Make me feel amazing
I love the way you touch me
Lick me
Nipples erect and ready
Make me lose control

Make me moan, make me groan
Take me to the Pleasuredome
Make love to me
Don't sex me!

Men Cry Too

Go ahead, cry,
You're allowed.
So what if you're loud
And outsiders hear?
Your vulnerability is sexy.
So, go ahead, cry.
Release those endorphins.
That stigma of being weak
Is total bullshit!
Crying reduces stress, and anxiety,
So, better out than in.
Just because you're a guy
Doesn't mean you shouldn't cry.
Yes, men don't cry, typically,
But we're now in the 21st century.
So, macho or not,
No judgement here.
Just a shoulder
Whenever you need to shed a tear.

Midnight Poetry

I am Cinderella, with pen,
Needing to write a masterpiece
In good time before the clock strikes midnight!
If I fail, my writings will not be how they should be;
They will be unclear.
I will have missed my opportunity
To be a poetry princess.
No sparkly shoes, or fancy dress.
So, for me to succeed,
I must write with haste, and speed.
For Midnight Poetry to be guaranteed,
This piece must be ready by 11:59pm.

One Last Dance

[Trigger warning: suicide]

I thought we were close, like sisters should be,
We told each other everything, usually,
But this time was different.
I had no idea!
She left me with questions
No-one else could answer.
Damn her,
I thought we were close!
The date was marked on the calendar,
But still, I had no clue,
Hadn't worked it out.
Thought it was for a special occasion,
A surprise, maybe for me or the family...
The weekend before that date
We partied hard,
Danced like crazy,
She seemed so happy.
And she was, in her own way.
She had one last dance
And then she was ready...
I came home to find her hanging, literally!
She'd taken her own life; set herself free.
She was my sister!
Up to her eyeballs in

Whatever was making her unhappy,
And I couldn't see it.
I couldn't help her.
She couldn't talk to me!
I've got over blaming myself.
I struggle with not seeing the signs, but
Sometimes, there just aren't any.
So, I'm over that now, too
'Cause there was nothing I could do.
She didn't let me in!
Mental health is fucked up.
I miss her so much.

One Touch

He makes every hair
On my body stand up
Senses ignited
Nipples excited
They stand to attention
Ready for action
Demanding to be sucked
Body in arousal mode
And ready to explode!
All this from one touch.

Pick Me!

Let's not make this any more complicated.
Shut up and hear me out.
You're gonna need to make a choice.
Don't want to be your afterthought.
We're caught up in this love triangle,
And I long to be at the summit.
Don't want to be piggy in the middle,
Or a gooseberry.
Three into two won't go,
And two into three is never equal,
So, you, me, her is irrational.
I'm sure she's cool, and nice, and funny,
But I love you!
I know I slap you one minute
And embrace you the next,
And you're right to be confused, but
That's just my wacky sense of humour.
So pick me, not her!
And let's get this love back on track.

Poems Never Written

Poems that are never written
Are words held captive, forbidden.
Expressions of feelings gone unsaid,
Held like prisoners in a cell.
Oh what shame, what sadness;
Better to put pen to paper
And create happiness.

Poem to a Stranger

"Hello.
Hi.
I've been watching you for a while.
Just love your smile.
No. No. I'm not a stalker.
It's just that I come here too, and
I've seen you
Sat on that same bench.
I've been meaning to say something, but
Wasn't sure how you'd feel
About someone invading your privacy.
Especially me, a stranger –
Someone you've never met, and don't know.
Please, if you'd rather be alone
Just say so, I won't be offended.
Maybe brokenhearted...
Now that I have your attention,
Is everything ok?
I see you've been crying.
I'm so very sorry.
I apologise for being so nosy.
It wasn't my intention to pry.
Just thought I could get to know you,
And you, me?
But it's cool if you'd rather have your own space.

I get that, and you know what,
I'm gonna leave You to You.
But, before I go,
And in case you don't already know,
That face is way too handsome to soil with tears.
Bye now.
Hoping to see you tomorrow."

Poetic Scars

Look at these marks on my skin
Poetic scars and bruises
Borne out of frustration
Trying to pen the perfect limerick
My heart bleeding, and broken
From sonnets of unrequited love
The scars vary in sizing
Some still fresh, others faint and healing
I refuse to let my pen fail
And inflict further scars
Because I'm fresh out of plasters
So with pen in hand, I continue
To find the perfect lyric or haiku
And when I do
All band aids will be off
And scars will start disappearing
'Cause I will have written the perfect poem

Postcard

He'd promised to send me one
From everywhere he stopped.
And there was the first,
In the palm of my hand.
The message was short, and sweet.
Not that one could get much on it.
And I was cool with that,
'Cause he was no Writer or Poet.
"I love and miss you," is what it said.
Brought a smile to my face.
And though I knew there'd be another postcard next week,
I couldn't wait to have him back from his business trip.

Secret

That was the plan.
It was!
Promised to tell him as soon as shit got serious.
But I'm still holding out.
Unsure how this will affect us,
But it will. I know it will!
How long can my relationship survive this secret?
The question is on repeat, yet,
I'm still unable to bring myself
To tell him.
So, on we go.
But for him, for me, for us,
I'm just gonna have to come clean,
And tell him I cheated.

She Walks in Beauty

All eyes should see her
This beautiful creature
She's the brightest of stars
Shining profusely
Lighting up dark nights
A sight for sore eyes
She walks with style
Elegantly, and with grace
Her face glowing
Her beauty striking
Radiance oozing from her head to her feet
She is angelic

Side Effects of Poetry

A poetry addict,
I'm lost without Sonnets.
Sometimes google-eyed from a Haiku
Or brokenhearted and feeling blue.
Other times, fits of giggles
From a humorous Limerick.
Sometimes nauseous, and feeling sick.
All symptoms of being starved of lyrics!
Dizzy,
Palms all sweaty,
Sleepless nights, anxiety,
All side effects of Poetry.
These are profound, but
I'll continue to work on a remedy.
In the meantime, I'll increase the dose.
What's the worst that can happen?

Soundtrack of Memories

You kiss my lips.
I look into your eyes and reminisce...
When we first met, I knew
I longed to be *Close to You.*
I fell in love and was *Crazy For You,*
Didn't wanna let you go,
Wanted to *Hold On* forever,
Not just one more day.
Simply had to stay, 'cause
Baby I Love Your Way.
Knew I'd found my *Real Love*
'Cause my dream came true.
Nothing Compares 2 U and never will!

Stop

We need to stop the gun crime,
Knife crime.
We need to find a solution
To defuse the situation.
It's far too depressing,
All this killing –
Gun crime,
Knife crime.
This needs to stop.
Youngers, listen up!
Life ain't about being a bad man,
It's about making the right decisions,
Negotiating your way out of sticky situations,
But without a weapon.
Being armed doesn't make you
A rude boy, or a bad man.
Nah Bro, it makes you a victim of circumstance,
But I understand.
Stereotypically falling into a system
Designed to keep you down,
Negatively portraying you through perception,
Expecting you to take the lives of your brethren…
And, you oblige.
Making you a statistic on the black hit list.
Youngers, you need to stop this!

End the cycle,
Retreat,
Relinquish,
Dashing away the guns don't make you weak.
Choose peace. Choose humanity. Choose harmony.
Choose love. Choose unity.
All lives matter.
Yours, mine, his, hers, theirs.
Too many families have shed tears
Over the loss of a young life,
Ended needlessly.
Sadly, this is reality.
Checked!
We need to stop the gun crime.
We need to stop the knife crime.
We need to wise up,
This needs to stop!
Arm yourself with wisdom;
Educate yourself on the traumas of history.
Let knowledge be your next victory.

I wrote this Poem in October 2022. Because of the message, I wanted it to reach as wide an audience as possible. I once again collaborated with @Broken_pen. The video has had many views. Check it out via this link:
https://www.instagram.com/reel/C1NWFqHMrpV/?igsh=MWl1OHVibncxbDF6MQ==

Suffer the Little Children...
[Trigger warning: child abuse]

If children are a blessing,
What was Sara Sharif?
What was Victoria Climbié?
What was Baby P?
What were all the others
Who met tragic ends
Through abuse and neglect?
Tortured,
Traumatised,
Bodies used as punching bags
Or ashtrays to stub out fags.
If children are a blessing, then
Why inflict such pain and suffering?
Innocent beings,
Pure,
Vulnerable,
Unsuspecting.
If children are a blessing...
What the fuck are Social Services servicing?
Hiding behind a desk,
A file,
Pen in hand.
Ticking boxes,
Crossing T's, dotting I's,

Coming across as caring,
Yet all the while
Children are dying.
Everyone knew, but no-one talked.
Everyone knew, but no-one connected the dots.
Shirking responsibility,
Evading accountability.
What cowards!
The system is flawed, and clearly not working.
But it's ok:
"We'll learn from this. It won't happen again."
If children are a blessing,
It shouldn't happen at all!

Tell Me How To Love You

When I think we're on track,
It's back to the starting line.
How do I keep getting this so wrong!
Am I not trying hard enough?
I want there to be an "us".
So in order to get this right,
I need you to tell me how to love you.

The Date...

The date was going good
Until my Ex showed up,
And right when we were ready to fuck!
I know I should've kept my mouth shut,
But I didn't expect him to follow us.
He and I spoke, you see,
And I told him about you and me,
How we'd be doing dinner, then
Heading home for a nightcap.

Now, here we are, naked and ready for action –
Only to be interrupted by a goddamn home invasion!
You right, I should have changed the locks;
You have every right to cuss,
But, please, don't leave.
I'm free next week...
Damn it!

The Hotel

We walk into the room.
First thing in view is a king-size.
Adrenaline starts pumping,
Nervous excitement, and
I'm shaking,
I'm beside myself,
So totally excited!
You and me, together, at last.
Been planning this for weeks
And now, here we are.
Lights turned down low,
Ambience set,
We cuddle; we kiss.
Each one more and more passionate.
Your hands get familiar,
Make their way down there!
Damn, it's getting hot in here...
Air con goes up a notch,
Hands go back to my crotch,
Clothes come off.
You're putting me on a high.
You're my sex drug,
My lovebug.

Just love our escapes to The Hotel,
Where we can get flirty and dirty,
And hide our infidelity.

The Keepsake

It hangs around my neck
It's my lucky charm
It protects me from harm
It's a daily reminder
Of the love we share
I wear it with pride
The keepsake you gave me
Will never leave my side!

The Park Bench

I see him, sat there,
He looks sad.
Deep in thought.
I want to ask: "Are you ok, Pops?"
But I don't. I nod instead,
He nods back,
A half-smile on his face.
It doesn't look forced,
So I feel he's ok?
I see a wedding band,
I assume he comes here
To free his mind.
Has wifey passed?
Is this their bench,
Where they used to sit?
And now he sits there, reminiscing?
I want to ask, but I don't.
Feel I may be intruding.
I give him a full smile, which I hope says
"I get it."
But I probably don't!
Maybe his world is as dark as his skin...

To My Future Love

And having been bitten once,
I'm shy and reserved.
Can you blame me?
Yet with all that said,
I'm happy to give love another chance.
I want to be wined, and dined, and romanced…
Just don't want another broken heart
So, to any future love of mine:
Be gentle, be romantic, be kind.

Toothpaste and Orange

I really wanted this!
Played the scene over and over in my head:
You, me, and a king-size bed.
Et, voila...
Just as I envisaged,
We did the nasty.
You popped the cherry –
Won't lie, the sex was fly.
Did things to me,
Made me moan, made me groan,
Put me on cloud nine,
And then some.
Now we're an item,
Boyfriend and girlfriend.
Sex became our serial
And everything else immaterial.
And though that was cool,
You started changing.
You became territorial,
Wanted to pin me down.
Where did this shit come from?
I needed time to think,
To soul search
And realise my worth.
The sex and you were sweet,

But my mental health meant so much more.
I am woman, watch me roar!
That's when it hit me.
Though this analogy may sound strange,
We're like Toothpaste and Orange.
Don't get me wrong,
I thoroughly enjoyed the journey,
But what I need is a Toothbrush,
Not Vitamin C!

Sayonara!

Unique

Hey there.
I'm a Poet!
Pretty sexy too,
Even if I self-proclaim.
When my pen takes aim,
I write to please,
Sometimes I tease.
Poetry is a breeze,
A breath of fresh air, and
Yes, I'm aware,
I'm lyrical,
Spiritual, 100!
A Dominican born and bred.
Hold the Republic.
I'm talking the Nature Isle –
365 rivers and a plethora of rainforests.
That's where I'm from!
UK-based
Since the age of 10,
London Town, to be exact.
But home is where the heart is
And mine is...
Thankful for all commodities
I now take for granted.
But my culture is deeply rooted!

Mum passed on when I was 19;
My world turned dark.
Heart akin to a crime scene.
Often ask how I'm still surviving.
It's been the hardest thing… but
Needed to trust the process.

Forty years on and I'm still here,
Making her proud, I hope.
Been a good girl;
Kept my eyes on the prize.
Confident, not cocky,
Pretty fucking dope actually!
Educated,
Sporty,
Gifted at penning poetry,
Blessed, and highly favoured.

A pretty cool human being.
Attentive to others,
Their well-being.
Caring.
Not boasting, just affirming.

My favourite part of me is me.
Simply,
Who I am.
Slam…
Dunk!

What Love is (1) ...

Cosy nights in,
Whispering sweet nothings.
Holding me tight,
So tight it's stifling,
Contented,
Happy,
Two peas in a pod.
A bond,
A love,
Passion,
Affection,
Finishing each other's sentences Intimacy.
You and me,
Us.
Love is precious,
Love is give and take,
Love is compromise.
Looking into each other's eyes,
Saying nothing,
The heart doing the talking.
Feelings so strong
They can't be ignored.
Lips locking,
Hands caressing,
Lovemaking

Till bodies ache
To the point of climax.
Love is all these things, and then some!

What Love Is (2) ...

Hearts beating in sync
Sweet nothings in my ear
Kisses on my lips
Slipping into something romantic
Bodies gyrating between the sheets
You may not agree with me,
But that's my kind of love!

When I Say What I Say

When I say I love you
Know it's more than just words
It's the things you do
It's everything about you
It's the way you make me feel, so,
When I say I love you...

Why Did You Tell Me?

Damned if you do and damned if you don't,
But why did you tell me?
You slept with her months ago
And you're telling me now?
All it's done is put me in limbo.
Do I stick or twist?
This was all so fucking unnecessary,
You dumb schmuck.
Ignorance is bliss.
I could have handled this,
But now I'm picturing
You and her together.
I loved you so much.
Thought things were good with us;
Never doubted your loyalty.
But now I'm questioning
Whether you ever loved me.
Was she so hard to resist
That once you started
You couldn't stop?
I gave you all of me.
Yet you still cheated.
You're a self-centred, arrogant,
Son of a bitch.
How dare you beg for forgiveness

After treating me like shit?
No doubt everything you said was a lie.
Were your feelings ever genuine?
I mean, if I did something wrong,
You should have said.
We could have spiced things up in bed.
But no, you fucked around instead.
And after nearly two months,
You tell me.
Did you need to?
This revelation has left me stunned.
But it's all good.
Get the fuck out.
We done!

Why Me – A Menopause Journey

First off, it's not just you.
It's every woman leaving 40
And hitting 50;
So, that's you, her, us, even me.
Sure, we all ask the question,
But rather than call out depression,
It's better to read up on this shit
And learn how best to deal with it!
After all, it's here to stay.
So, why stress over a process
Neither you nor I can stop?
It will happen, and when it does,
Let's meet it head on.
And look on the bright side,
No more pads or fucking tampons!

Willing

I was willing to keep us going,
Was in it for the long haul,
For the rough,
The smooth, and
Everything else in between.
But you had other ideas.
You flipped us.
Did a full 360.
Now you're back with your Ex.
I hope you're both really happy.
And though I hold no grudge,
And should have seen
What was right in front of me,
I think I deserved the truth!

Yes, You Can!

When you think you can't,
When your days look dark,
When the outcome seems bleak,
When you think you can't –
Think again,
Take the reins,
You're the captain of this ship.
You got this.
When you think you can't –
Yes, you can!

You Are the Story

Been thinking of my next novel.
There'll be a hero,
A knight in shining armour.
He'll be suave and debonair –
Tall, and dark, and handsome.
He'll need to rescue a damsel in distress,
And probably a whole lot more.
I'm unsure of other characters
And thicker plot,
'Cause it's still a work in progress.
But it starts and ends with you,
'Cause you are the story.